G(

THE UNLIKELY

30 DAY DEVOTIONAL SERIES ON
THE PEOPLE OF THE BIBLE

JON DYER

TABLE OF CONTENT

Introduction:
God Chooses the Unlikely

Key Passage: *"Brothers and sisters, think of what you were when you were called. Not many of you were wise by human standards; not many were influential; not many were of noble birth. But God chose the foolish things of the world to shame the wise; God chose the weak things of the world to shame the strong. God chose the lowly things of this world and the despised things – and the things that are not – to nullify the things that are, so that no one may boast before him. It is because of him that you are in Christ Jesus, who has become for us wisdom from God – that is, our righteousness, holiness and redemption. Therefore, as it is written: 'Let the one who boasts boast in the Lord.'"* 1 Corinthians 1:26-31

Recycling: Taking what could be trash and making it into something useful.

Repurposing: Taking something that is not useful and making it useful for another purpose.

Reconditioning: Taking something old and remaking it to be useful for its original purpose.

Remodeling: Tearing out the old parts of a home and rebuilding it with modern amenities.

In our modern culture, it has become fashionable to be environmentally friendly. We are rightfully taught not to waste but to recycle. There are numerous TV shows depicting creative uses for all kinds of trash, whether it be restoring cars, refurbishing homes, or revitalizing furniture. We are encouraged to salvage and utilize rather than waste, and when we do well, we exhibit great pride in our ingenuity.

God has been doing these very same things from the beginning of time with people. He recycles the worn out and remakes them to accomplish great tasks for His glory. He repurposes the broken as He calls them to Himself and gives them Kingdom work. He reconditions the weary with new energy and assigns them to do what others see as impossible. He remodels lives that are worn down through mistakes and rebuilds people into valuable vessels in His hands.

In the devotions that follow, we will encounter people throughout the Bible and discuss how God used these people. They were real people, just like us, with flaws, weaknesses, and sketchy pasts. Despite that, God chose them and used them anyway to face impossible odds. In fact, God seldom chooses those who are most likely to succeed. Instead, He loves to work through outcasts and underdogs: the unlikely options.

Why does God so often choose the most unlikely of heroes in His plan? Because when the unlikely succeed, His glory is revealed. Everyone around can see that God must have been working in the least among them, because they were too broken to do anything on their own. When God uses people who the world considers useless, God gets the credit and the glory. Time after time we see this play out in Scripture as God chooses to work through the humblest of people to do great things. This is God's pattern throughout the Bible.

God still works the same way today. He takes the weak and downtrodden and wins incredible victories for His kingdom through them. You may feel like you have nothing to offer God's Kingdom because of your past, a disability, your age, or gender. If so, remember: God uses the unlikely. It is when you think you have little or nothing to offer to God that you are the perfect candidate to do beautiful, amazing, and miraculous things for God's glory. When He uses you, He will be the One that gets the credit and you will have no option but to point to Him. That is exactly how God wants it.

As you approach these devotions, recognize that God remakes and uses the most unlikely to do the most amazing things. He will transform your life too, if you will allow Him. If you need to be recycled, repurposed, reconditioned or remodeled, God is just the One to accomplish that in you as He works through you. Hold on, because wherever you are in life God is not finished with you yet.

Day 1
Paul – God Overcomes Your Past

Key Passage: *"If someone else thinks they have reasons to put confidence in the flesh, I have more: circumcised on the eighth day, of the people of Israel, of the tribe of Benjamin, a Hebrew of Hebrews; in regard to the law, a Pharisee; as for zeal, persecuting the church; as for righteousness based on the law, faultless. But whatever were gains to me I now consider loss for the sake of Christ."* Philippians 3:4b-7

Everyone has a past. It would be great if we were totally comfortable with our past and able to live without regrets. The problem is we all have regrets. We all make decisions we wish we could redo. There are so many mistakes that leave us ashamed. In our guilt, we try to bury our actions, but they keep coming back to haunt us. What is done can't be undone.

Paul is one of the great heroes of the Bible. It's hard to imagine anyone besides Jesus who had more of an influence on Christianity than Paul. From the beginning of Paul's life, it seemed he was set up to succeed. Scholars believe His father was a Roman general or administrator, explaining why he was granted the privilege of Roman citizenship from birth.

His devout Jewish parents raised him in the important port city of Tarsus and ensured Paul grew up with the elite of society. He was taught by the leading Rabbis of the time and undoubtedly memorized all 613 Jewish commandments and much of the Old Testament: *"a Hebrew of Hebrews"*. Yet this is just the first half of Paul's story.

When we meet Paul in Acts, his religious life and zeal was blinding him to the truth. In 1 Timothy 1:13 he writes, *"I was once a blasphemer and a persecutor and a violent man ... I acted in ignorance and unbelief."* Paul had been taught that Jesus and his followers were against God and so Paul obtained permission to persecute the early Church at home and abroad. We know that as the crowd stoned Stephen, Paul cheered them on and held their coats. Paul's goal was to wipe out Christians everywhere because, at that time, he believed it was the right thing to do.

Have you ever believed something so strongly that it blinded you from seeing the truth? When examining Paul's story, we can see the power of God to change a life. God took a man who intensely persecuted the Church and, by His grace, transformed him[1]. Paul became a man who spread the good news throughout the world and wrote much of the New Testament. Furthermore, God used his upbringing amongst the Gentiles combined with his Jewish education to enable Paul to effectively bring the gospel "first to the Jew, then to the Gentile"[2].

If your life is full of regret and you are ashamed of the things you've done, remember Paul. Jesus has the power to completely turn your life around, cleanse you, and give you a new start. He is the only one who can heal a sinful past. God promises to blot out your mistakes and, even more amazingly, He promises in Joel 2:25 to *"repay you for the years the locusts have eaten."*

Related Passages:

1. Galatians 1:13

2. Romans 1:16

3. Acts 9

4. Acts 22:6-28

5. Galatians 1:15-16

6. Philippians 3:4-5

Day 2
Gideon - God Encourages the Fearful

Key Passage: *"When the angel of the Lord appeared to Gideon, he said 'The Lord is with you, mighty warrior.'"* Judges 6:12

With the ongoing threat of terrorism, wars, epidemics and natural disasters in the world today, there are more people afraid than ever. Uncertainty makes us all fearful. On a more personal level, we dread the daily stresses of rejection, failure, and loneliness.

We first meet Gideon threshing wheat in a winepress, trying to save what he could of his harvest. He was scared, frightened, defeated, and thus in hiding. Usually, people would thresh wheat in a field so the wind could carry away the outer husk, but Gideon was down a hole in the ground for fear the Midianites would steal his grain.

The Midianites were an enemy with sinister strategy. They would let Israel do all the work plowing, planting, and weeding the fields right up until they were ready to harvest. Then, at last minute, they would raid the Israelite villages and steal the harvest.

As Judges 6:5 says, *"The [Midianites] came up with their livestock and their tents like swarms of locusts. It was impossible to count them or their camels; they invaded the land to ravage it."*

Knowing what Gideon faced, it's easy for us to understand why he was hiding. Gideon had gone year after year of working the land and expecting a harvest, just for him to have it stolen. Can you imagine the disappointment he felt every year as it happened again and again? It's amazing that he chose not to give up. Instead he still planted his fields time after time.

Yet, when the angel of the LORD appears to Gideon, he calls him *"a mighty warrior."* God looks at this defeated young man in hiding and, despite seeing his situation, his weakness, and his fear, he also sees the potential in Gideon to lead Israel against the Midianites. In the conversation that follows, Gideon continually doubts God's word and promises. He asks God to prove Himself over and over again. By pure grace, God confirms His promises and choses to bolster Gideon's faith.[1]

God goes on to reduce Gideon's thirty-two-thousand-man army to three-hundred to show that better physical circumstances are not the solution to our fear and to demonstrate that it is God who gives us victory. However, Gideon is still fearful of failure, so God wakes him up in the middle of the night and tells him to go into the enemy's camp. Gideon overhears the enemy saying *"God has given the Midianites and the whole camp into [Gideon's] hands."*[2] While Gideon may have feared failure, the enemy feared Gideon because they recognized that God had already granted him victory.

We, like Gideon, can be so affected by our fear and past experiences that we doubt God's promises to us. Often, we read a passage in the Bible or hear a message and conclude that it cannot be meant for us. We're too insignificant and cowardly for God to be calling us! We tell God that we must be the wrong person for the job.

God says to Gideon and us *"Go in the strength you have... Am I not sending you? I will be with you."* God continues to show Gideon that the only thing he needs is the presence of God with him. Psalm 27:1 says, *"The LORD is my light and my salvation– whom shall I fear? The LORD is the stronghold of my life– of whom shall I be afraid?"* God teaches us through Gideon that the only correct perspective of our problem is to see it from God's perspective. He is the almighty and nothing is too difficult for God.

Related Passages:

1. Judges 6:1-16

2. Judges 6:33-40

3. Judges 7:14

4. Jeremiah 32:37

Day 3
Noah – God Honors the Faithful

Key Passage: *"By faith Noah, when warned about things not yet seen, in holy fear built an ark to save his family. By his faith he condemned the world and became heir of the righteousness that is in keeping with faith."* Hebrews 11:7

It is difficult to be different. By our nature, we want to blend in and be popular. How many people have attended a party they knew was a bad idea, but when invited did not want to seem impolite by saying no? How many businessmen have made dodgy business deals to impress their colleagues? The truth is most of us have compromised our standards or beliefs at one time or another to gain merit with other people.

Noah lived in an age where *"every inclination of the thoughts of the human heart was only evil all the time."*[1] It had become so bad that God regretted creating mankind. Yet in the midst of all this Genesis 6:9 tell us, *"Noah was a righteous man, blameless among the people of his time, and he walked faithfully with God."* Noah didn't compromise with his culture but lived to honour God.

When God called Noah to build an ark, I can imagine

that he wondered if he was up to the task. I know I would have. The complexity of what God was asking him to do was enormous. He would have to source the right trees, prepare them to be worked, then measure, cut, and assemble them into the ark before sealing the boat to make it waterproof. He would have to be an engineer, carpenter, and animal keeper. If building a boat 137 meters long (450ft) was not difficult enough, he also had to fill it with animals. Lions, snakes, elephants, scorpions, spiders, wolves and insects - at least two of every living creature on the surface of the earth needed to get on the ark. Not only would Noah have to build pens to house them, but he would have to feed, water and clean up after them for as long as the earth was flooded. It took Noah somewhere between 55 years to 120 years to build the Ark. This was no easy, short-term task, but rather his life's calling.

For all those years, you can imagine the ridicule people were heaping upon him. While everyone else was living large and doing whatever they pleased, Noah was spending his days working hard sawing wood. In a time period which had never seen rain, Noah was building a huge inland boat simply because God had told him to construct an ark.

People will often think we are crazy when we chose to honor God with our lives. When God calls us to something it often does not make sense to those around us. When God told the disciples to cast their nets after not catching anything all night, it didn't make sense. When the missionary David Livingstone left Scotland for Africa and to suffer incredible hardship, sickness, hunger, hostile tribes, lion attacks and the loss of his wife to malaria, his actions didn't make sense to many. Yet Livingstone, was responding to the higher calling to preach the gospel and the fruit of his faithfulness lives on until today.

It took courage for Noah to build an ark in the face of popular opinion and to continue to preach for 120 years when the only people who believed his message was his family[3]. Nevertheless, Noah's faithfulness to God's calling saved his family and ultimately the human race. If God has called you to do something, He is the One who verifies it. Don't compromise his calling for popularity, comfort, or ease. Respond faithfully like Noah, and trust God to produce great fruit.

Related Passages:

1. Genesis 6:5

2. Hebrews 11:7

3. 2 Peter 2:5

Day 4
Leah - God Loves the Heartbroken

Key Passage: *"Leah became pregnant and gave birth to a son. She named him Reuben, for she said, 'It is because the LORD has seen my misery. Surely my husband will love me now.' She conceived again, and when she gave birth to a son she said, 'Because the LORD heard that I am not loved, he gave me this one too.' So she named him Simeon. Again she conceived, and when she gave birth to a son she said, 'Now at last my husband will become attached to me, because I have borne him three sons.' So he was named Levi. She conceived again, and when she gave birth to a son she said, 'This time I will praise the LORD.' So she named him Judah. Then she stopped having children."* Genesis 29:32-35

It is terrible to feel unloved or in second place. Yet, it's pretty common. We all have experienced abandonment or neglect. It could be in the form of a friend who rejects you for another, or a parent who walks out the door and never comes back, or hearing your sibling be continually praised while your achievements are overlooked. You may love a boyfriend, girlfriend, husband, or wife who doesn't love you back. We know the heartache and we understand the wound that the callousness of others leaves behind. After a while, we can start to believe we are not worthy of love: we are undesirable, a hindrance and a problem. Some eventually conclude that the world would be better off without them. This is a lie of the Enemy, as we can see through Leah's life. The Bible is clear! 1 John 4:9-10 says, *"This is how God showed his love among us: He sent his one and only Son into the world that we might live through him. This is love: not that we loved God, but that he loved us and sent his Son as an atoning sacrifice for our sins."*

As we read the story of Leah in the Bible, we can't help but sympathize with her. Despite being the older sister, she was regularly passed over for her younger sister, Rachel. The Bible describes Leah as "weak-eyed." Whether this is referring to her appearance or poor eyesight we no longer know, but we can understand the difficulty she faced to live up to the standard set by the "lovely figure" of her younger sister. Leah had grown up living in that shadow, and even in her married life, she could not escape it since her husband, Jacob, was also married and head over heels in love with her sister, Rachel. She loved Jacob, but he didn't love her back. We can feel her heartache.

Jacob never really wanted Leah, but was tricked by her father into marrying her. You can imagine the conversation when Jacob found out! While Jacob kept up a public show for the honeymoon week, it was obvious to everyone what was going on when he married Rachel as soon as Leah's one short week was over. Imagine going through your honeymoon knowing your husband is just counting down the days until he can marry your sister! The week of neglect turned into years. Jacob and Rachel made Leah feel like the proverbial unwanted third wheel. They thought she was in the way and they would be better off without her.

Leah might have been forgotten and unloved by her family, but she was not forgotten or unloved by God. Leah gave birth to six sons and a daughter. She gave birth to Jacob's firstborn, Reuben. Another of her sons, Judah, would be the ancestor of the royal family of Israel. Levi's line became the priests and teachers for all of Israel. We know Leah recognized that this was God's favour to her, based on the way she named her children:

- Reuben: *"the LORD has seen my misery,"*
- Simeon: *"the LORD heard that I am not loved,"*
- Judah: *"I will praise the LORD."*

Unlike Leah, we often fail to see God's hand of favour in our lives when we feel unloved. God knows your heartache and loves you dearly. Even if others treat you as second best, God loves you and has a plan to use you and bless you. Keep your focus on Him and his love, and leave the rest to God.

Related Passages:

1. 1 John 4:9-10

2. John 3:16

Day 5
Joseph – God Restores the Abandoned

Key Passage: *"You intended to harm me, but God intended it for good to accomplish what is now being done, the saving of many lives."* Genesis 50:20

In life, we are faced with many choices, but the one thing that none of us chose is our family. No one gave us the option of which parents we would have, how wealthy we would be, or where we were born. We were all born into different sets of circumstances without any say whatsoever.

Joseph was born into a chosen family. His parents loved him deeply. In fact, as unfair as it sounds, he was their favorite child. This favoritism caused his brothers to resent him to the point of hatred.

Like many today, Joseph was born into a split family or half family. While they all shared the same father, most of his half-siblings were sons born by Leah, Joseph's Aunt. She was unloved by Jacob, which probably made his brother's resentment even worse. When Joseph was seventeen years old, his mother, Rachel, died. Instead of comforting their brother, his half-siblings decided it was payback time.

Things started to go from bad to worse for Joseph. When his father, Jacob, sent Joseph to visit his brothers he probably was not excited since he knew they did not like him. He had already experienced their bullying, but he probably wasn't expecting what came next. Genesis 37:18 says *"But [Joseph's brothers] saw him in the distance, and before he reached them, they plotted to kill him."* What a welcome! However, just before they were going to leave him to die of thirst in a hole in the ground, they see some slave traders and realize they can both get rid of Joseph and make some money at the same time.

Joseph was tied up and dragged to Egypt. Through the hot desert sun, every step took him further from his father who loved him. Every step reminded him that his own brothers had sold him into slavery.

When Joseph got to Egypt, he was sold to a man named Potiphar, who after time, saw Joseph's value and put him in charge of all his household. Time passed, and Potiphar's wife began to lust after Joseph. He honored God and refused her advances, so she lied to get Joseph thrown into prison. Once again, Joseph is mistreated and abandoned. Even in prison, when his fellow inmates promise to remember him after their release, they forget to mention him to Pharaoh, the ruler of Egypt. Time after time, Joseph is mistreated, abandoned and forgotten by those who are close to him.

We know the rest of the account. In God's perfect timing, Joseph is remembered and correctly interprets Pharaoh's dreams. To honor the man obviously blessed by God, Pharaoh promotes Joseph from his prison cell to ruler of Egypt, second only to Pharaoh himself.

Throughout all the years of mistreatment and abandonment, God was shaping Joseph like a piece of clay. Everything he had gone through was preparing him for the day he suddenly oversaw a country. Nothing occurs in our life by accident; God uses everything to shape us.

Joseph went on to save not only Egypt from a drought, but also his brothers who had treated him so disgracefully. God gave Joseph an amazing understanding of his own life, because when he does finally see his brothers again, he is able to tell them, *"You intended to harm me, but God intended it for good to accomplish what is now being done, the saving of many lives."*[1]

If you have been mistreated, it can be incredibly difficult to trust anyone again, let alone forgive those that wronged you. Maybe you find yourself in an emotional prison. Let Joseph remind you that God delights to deliver people from dark places and use them to save many.

Related Passages:

1. Genesis 50:20

2. Romans 8:28

3. Jeremiah 29:11

4. Genesis 37

Day 6
Samson – God Overcomes
Mid-life Crisis

Key Passage: *"The woman gave birth to a boy and named him Samson. He grew and the LORD blessed him, and the Spirit of the LORD began to stir him while he was in Mahaneh Dan, between Zorah and Eshtaol." Judges 13:24-25*

Samson stands out as one of the notable people of the Bible. His name even means 'shining like the sun'. Samson is the Biblical hero that all the boys in Sunday School want to be. He has been called the Hebrew Hercules, fighting lions with his bare hands, tearing up gates made to withstand an army, and pulling down a temple. What strength, what a hero!

Samson had a blessed childhood. His godly parents sought God's instruction on how to raise him and set a good example for him[1]. They were not hypocritical, asking Samson to do as they said, not as they did. He was raised a Nazarite, taking a pledge to abstain from fleshly desires so he would stand out in the crowd as someone dedicated to God. He had enormous physical strength; a gift from the Spirit of God. In fact, the Holy Spirit is mentioned more in the story of

Samson than the rest of the Book of Judges combined.

However, Samson faced a battle that we all face. Often, we master one area of our life only to fail in another. We manage our finances well, but not our health. We invest in our work life, but not our marriage. We keep our anger under control, but not our greed.

As Samson hits middle age, he begins to give into his lusts and compromise his vows. After twenty years of oppression by the Philistines who were ruling the land, he decides to marry one. The marriage doesn't even happen, as his wife is given away to one her Philistine friends after Samson loses his temper. Then comes along Delilah, who tricks him time and time again. Eventually, she cuts his hair and hands him over to the enemy. After years of spiritual neglect Judges 16:20 says, *"He awoke from his sleep and thought, 'I'll go out as before and shake myself free.' But he did not know that the LORD had left him."*

When the Philistines finally capture Samson, they do not kill him; rather they blind him and keep him prisoner so they can mock him. On the great feast day for their idol, Dagon, the Philistines bring Samson into the temple to mock him further. Instead, Samson prays to the LORD, *"Sovereign LORD, remember me. Please, God, strengthen me just once more, and let me with one blow get revenge on the Philistines for my two eyes."*[2]. God grants his request and that day becomes his greatest victory. God alone can take your darkest hour of defeat and turn it into your hour of greatest victory.

Many of us, like Samson, lose the zeal we first had for God. Over time, we too begin to compromise with the world until we become just like them. Maybe you can remember how God used to use you, but now think you have drifted too far to be used again. Perhaps you believe the sin you've committed since becoming a believer separates you from God. The lesson we learn from Samson is that God is only a prayer away.

Related Passages:

1. Judges 13:8

2. Judges 16:20-28

Day 7
Elijah – God Meets the Depressed

Key Passage: *"[Elijah] came to a broom bush, sat down under it and prayed that he might die. 'I have had enough, Lord,' he said. 'Take my life; I am no better than my ancestors.' Then he lay down under the bush and fell asleep."* 1 Kings 19:4

It is estimated that depression affects 350 million people in the world today. Unfortunately, it can be a taboo subject within the church. We often have a stereotype of the perfect Christian as always happy and smiling. Consequently, when we fail to fit this personality type, we feel even more guilty and ashamed and so the downward spiral continues.

You may be surprised to know that depression is a recurrent theme throughout the Bible, the prophet Elijah being just one example. Despite being used powerfully by God and experiencing miracle after miracle, he goes from an amazing spiritual high to the deepest of lows.

In 1 Kings 17:1, Elijah proclaims a drought. He is taken to a solitary place, fully dependent on God. There

Elijah was fed twice every day by a miracle. When the brook eventually dried up Elijah experiences another miracle. He meets a widow ready to prepare her last meal with her last bit of flour and oil before starving to death with her son. God multiplies the flour and oil, so that each meal there is just enough for another. Throughout the drought, it never ran out, feeding Elijah, the lady and her son[1]. Sometime later, the son of the woman became ill, and finally stopped breathing. Elijah picked up the dead boy, carried him up to his room, *"stretched himself out on the boy three times and cried out to the LORD"* and God brought the boy back to life[1].

It doesn't end here! On returning to his homeland, he calls the people to decide whom they will serve. It was Elijah versus four hundred and fifty prophets of Baal. They agree that whomever calls down fire from Heaven to consume a sacrifice will have his god declared the true God. Elijah lets the prophets of Baal offer their sacrifice first. He is so confident that God will answer his prayer, that Elijah even mocks the prophets of Baal when nothing happens. When it is his turn, Elijah fearlessly insists that they pour water all over his wood three times before he prays to God for fire. God answer Elijah's prayer and fire falls from Heaven, even consuming the stone altar under the sacrifice.

At this point, Elijah has experienced God working supernaturally through him time and time again. He is the last person we would expect to become depressed, yet he does. The contrast between 1 Kings 18 and 1 Kings 19 is remarkable. In chapter 18, Elijah is courageous and confident above all odds. In chapter 19, he is crying to God asking God to take his life. This goes to show that depression can sneak up on anyone at any age.

Is that not how depression works? One moment everything seems to be great: we are on the top of the mountain. Then all of the sudden we find ourselves at the bottom of the valley with a dark cloud over us that we cannot outrun. All thought of victory and pass achievements fade and we are stuck in a restless state with no clear way out. For all the triumphs that Elijah had seen, he felt a failure and wanted it all to be over.

However, God does not abandon Elijah to his depression, but meets him there. He provides him with sleep, one of the things which is proven to help depression, but oh so hard to get when suffering from depression. God sends an angel to speak to him and food for him to eat. Then, on a mountain, God gives Elijah what we all need and long for: the living presence of God. Elijah is recommissioned and told to anoint Elisha. In the future, Elijah would become a mentor to Elisha and Elisha would become a great comfort to Elijah.

Maybe you identify with Elijah. Perhaps you too are struggling with feelings of worthlessness, guilt, anxiety, and failure. If you feel stuck in a dark valley, worthless and a failure, be sure God has not given up on you. Keep your eye on Him, and listen for the gentle whisper of his presence. God has great things in store for you, no matter how hard that might be to believe right now.

Related Passages:

1. 1 Kings 17:1-24

2. 1 Kings 19:15-21

Day 8
Abraham – God Has Perfect Timing

Key Passage: *"Against all hope, Abraham in hope believed and so became the father of many nations, just as it had been said to him, 'So shall your offspring be.' Without weakening in his faith, he faced the fact that his body was as good as dead—since he was about a hundred years old—and that Sarah's womb was also dead. Yet he did not waver through unbelief regarding the promise of God, but was strengthened in his faith and gave glory to God, being fully persuaded that God had power to do what he had promised."* Romans 4:18-21

Old age has a way of sneaking up on us. Regardless of your current age, I am sure you look back and wonder where the years went. The thought of becoming old is a scary thing for many people. It often comes along with deteriorating physical and mental health, more aches and pain, and worst of all, the loss of loved ones.

Abraham is noted for his faith in God which eventually saw him becoming the 'Father of many Nations.' Indeed, today we know he is the father of two people groups and three major world religions. However, what I love most about Abraham is that he is so much like us. His life was full of ups and downs. One moment he is doing great and the next he has messed up again. He demonstrates great moments of faith which are followed by stupid choices.

God promised Abraham that his descendants would be as numerous as the stars in the sky, and Genesis tells us that Abraham believed God. Yet as the years went by he decided that he had better help God out and took matters into his own hands. When Abraham was eighty-six years old, he sleeps with his wife's slave, Ishmael is born, and Abraham enters thirteen years of silence from God. Thirteen years! Abraham was probably wondering if he had finally messed up one too many times, causing him to miss out on what God had planned.

When Abraham was ninety-nine years old and all hope was gone, God finally appeared to him and said in Genesis 17, *"I am God Almighty; walk before me faithfully and be blameless. Then I will make my covenant between me and you and will greatly increase your numbers."*

Abraham was 100 years old when his son Isaac was born. Hebrews 11:12 says, *"And so from this one man, and he as good as dead, came descendants as numerous as the stars in the sky and as countless as the sand on the seashore."* He was so old that the writer of Hebrews refers to Abraham as 'good as dead.' Sarah, Abraham's wife, was around 90 years old when she had Isaac. Even with today's modern medicine this has never been accomplished. Impossible with man, but possible with God.

No matter how old we are, God can still use us to fulfil his purposes on earth. Regardless of your age, you have a vital role to play in the Church, and we need you. Even if you've been waiting years for God's promise to be fulfilled, keep trusting. Abraham was 100 years old when his promise from God was fulfilled. Anna was at least 84 when she met Jesus after years of waiting in the temple. Don't give up! Keep serving, and trust that God will honour His promises to you. The psalmist prayed, in Psalm 71:18 *"Even when I am old and gray, do not forsake me, my God, till I declare your power to the next generation, your mighty acts to all who are to come."* May that be a prayer for all of us.

Related Passages:

1. Genesis 15:6

2. Genesis 17:1-2

3. Psalm 71

Day 9
Timothy – God Works
Through the Young

Key Passage: *"Don't let anyone look down on you because you are young, but set an example for the believers in speech, in conduct, in love, in* faith *and in purity."* 1 Timothy 4:12

For those of us who do not feel too old, we probably feel too young, and there usually is no gap in between. Have you noticed how children always want to be one year older and love to say, "I am nearly..." Equally, many young adults live by the motto, "I am too young to settle down and commit to a relationship" only to directly move onto, "I am too old to get married, it's too late for me now."

Whether we like it or not, people judge us on our age. We had a small fire at the Christian centre where I work, and when the firemen came to put it out, they looked so young. So much so, a man watching from the street commented on how young they were. But the truth is, when experts like firefighters, police officers, teachers or doctors look young, we are probably getting old. The question is, do we show the same respect to a young professional as we would to an older professional?

This was the situation Timothy faced. Timothy had been traveling and ministering with Paul for a decade before Paul sent him alone to the church at Ephesus. While he was physically young, he had much spiritual maturity to offer. The problem was that people did not trust him because of his youth. The older generation looked down on him, thinking that their years of practical experience was worth more than his spiritual guidance.

When Paul writes to Timothy and tells him to not *"let anyone look down on you because you are young,"* he is reminding Timothy that age is no restriction to God. Whether young or old, God calls you to set an example. Timothy was not the only young person God used. David was just a boy when he defeated Goliath. King Josiah was eight when he became king and made a difference in Judah. The young boy who had two fish and five loaves didn't seem to have much to offer, but when he gave it all to Jesus, it fed 5,000 men, plus women and children.

Do not let your own, or other people's, perspective of your age restrict you, but set an example of faith and purity for all believers.

Related Passages:

1. 2 Kings 22

2. 1 Samuel 17

3. Philippians 2:19-24

4. 1 Corinthians 4:17

Day 10
Rahab – God Redeems
Sexual Sin

Key Passage: *"By faith the prostitute Rahab, because she welcomed the spies, was not killed with those who were disobedient."* Hebrews 11:31

Rahab is introduced to us in Joshua 2:1 as a prostitute. Not only is her profession undesirable, but she a Canaanite, one of the Israelites' enemies. There are numerous reasons why people get into prostitution. For some, it could be for money, either as an attempt to get rich or pay for a drug habit, but there are also those who have been caught in the sex trade and are held as slaves. Horrifically, many of these are young girls kidnapped from their families.

This may have been the case with Rahab. The people in Canaan worshipped a god called Ashtoreth, the goddess of sensual love. In her temple, there were many priestess who served Ashtoreth through prostitution. These were often chosen at a young age by the priest to serve in one of their temples. Whether Rahab was chosen to be a 'priestess of prostitution,' or became a common woman of the night, we know that she was living in sin.

Physically, she was living in a good place. Her house was on the walls of Jericho. Jericho was surrounded by two walls, both thirty feet high. The outer wall was six feet thick, and the inner wall was twelve feet thick. The house where Rahab lived would have been envied like a secure apartment with a view is today. There was security there; no one expected that the walls would be the first thing to fall.

However, deep down in Rehab's heart, she knew she was not safe. She had heard what the God of the Hebrews had done to bring His people out of Egypt. Consequently, by faith Rahab received the spies into her house to give them refuge and ask that they spare her family. Hebrews 11:31 tells us, *"By faith the prostitute Rahab, because she welcomed the spies, was not killed with those who were disobedient."*

I am sure there were other places the spies could have hid. I am sure there were many people in Jericho that we would consider more righteous than Rahab. Yet God considered all those other people disobedient, and they died while Rahab's faith saved her and her family. We, like Rahab, are also saved by grace, through faith – a gift from God[1]. We must not forget that Jesus came to save sinners.

Having a less than desirable profession does not mean that God can't use you for His glory. Rahab was a prostitute, David was a simple shepherd boy in the field, Matthew was a tax collector, and James and John were humble fishermen, yet each of them transformed the world for the glory of God. You may not be involved in a 'sinful' profession such as a prostitute or drug dealer, but you may still allow your profession to define you. Maybe you think, I am only a janitor, only a waiter, or only a garbage man. God would never use me like He would someone else. Look again at Rahab. She went on to marry an Israelite named Salmon and later became the mother of Boaz. Boaz married Ruth and became David's great-grandfather. While she did not know it at the time, Rahab would be one of Jesus' ancestors.

There is a great encouragement here for us. Regardless of low or how high our social standing may be, our profession does not define who we are or if God can use us. It is our faith in God that define us and by which we are saved. If you feel worthless and dirty or proud and safe high up on the walls, remember that wherever you are, the only safe place to be is in Christ!

Related Passages:

1. Ephesians 2:8

2. Matthew 1

Day 11
Job – God Teaches Through Loss

Key Passage: *"At this, Job got up and tore his robe and shaved his head. Then he fell to the ground in worship and said:*

> *'Naked I came from my mother's womb,*
>   *and naked I will depart.*
> *The Lord gave and the Lord has taken away;*
>   *may the name of the Lord be praised.'*

In all this, Job did not sin by charging God with wrongdoing." Job 1:20-22

What do people say about you when you are not listening? Often the only time we really know what people think of us is when we overhear a conversation. In Job 1, we are invited to observe a conversation between God and Satan. In Job 1:8 God says to Satan, *"Have you considered my servant Job? There is no one on earth like him; he is blameless and upright, a man who fears God and shuns evil."*

Oh, what a compliment for anyone to say about us, let alone have God say we are blameless! Job is also described as being *"the greatest man among all the people of the East"* as well as extremely wealthy, owning *"seven thousand sheep, three thousand camels, five hundred* yoke *of oxen and five hundred donkeys, and a large number of servants."*[1] God had also blessed him with seven sons and three daughters. Job's love for them and God caused him to sacrifice a burnt offering for each of his children every day, just in case they had sinned against God.

As we read Chapter 1 of Job, it's hard to imagine anyone who has faced a day like the one Job had. When Job woke up that day, he had no idea what the day would hold. Despite only ever seeking to honor God, in a matter of minutes, Job faces catastrophe after catastrophe without any idea why they are happening. First, he loses his many herds of livestock, along with the servants tending them, before finally hearing his very children are dead. The pain of losing a child must be terrible, but imagine losing ten children at once! Our heart can't but help but break for Job and his wife.

Having lost everything and mourning for his children, he next became ill and covered in terrible sores. His wife decides she has had enough and tells Job to *"curse God and die!"*[2]. In the following chapters his friends arrive, only to continue to give him bad advice. Despite all that has happened to him, Job still chooses to worship the God who has allowed all his loss to happen.

Job had much. He was most likely the wealthiest man alive in his day and with a lovely family too boot. Yet, his hope, trust, and security were in nothing other than God alone. Maybe you too have lost something precious. Many people's lives are turned upside down when they lose their jobs, children, or marriage. I've spoken with many a successful person who has ended up living on the streets. Maybe you've lost the health that you used to enjoy and take for granted. Job is an amazing testimony of someone who never loses his faith in God even when losing everything else. In Job 19:25 he proclaims, *"I know that my redeemer lives, and that in the end, he will stand on the earth."*

Following Jesus doesn't guarantee us an easy and comfortable life, but it does give us a firm, secure anchor for our souls. If you have lost something dear to you, it does not mean God has ceased to love you. Neither does it mean that you have messed up nor that He is not working in you even now for His glory. When we hurt it can be hard to see how God is moving in our lives. However, that is when it is the most important for us to trust in his faithfulness and unfailing love. God does not give up on anyone, even if they walk in the valley of the shadow of death.

Related Passages:

1. Job 1:3

2. Job 2:9

3. Hebrews 6:19

Day 12
Moses – God Conquers
Physical Disability

Key Passage: *"'Pardon your servant, Lord. I have never been eloquent, neither in the past nor since you have spoken to your servant. I am slow of speech and tongue.' 'Who gave human beings their mouths? Who makes them deaf or mute? Who gives them sight or makes them blind? Is it not I, the LORD? Now go; I will help you speak and will teach you what to say.'"* Exodus 4:10-12

Moses life did not start out well. He was born in Egypt during the time when Pharaoh had decreed all Hebrew baby boys were to be killed at birth. You probably know the story well. His parents hid him for the first three months, before placing him in the Nile river. Pharaoh's daughter saw him floating in the water and adopted him into her family. Moses was educated in Egypt's finest schools where he was taught all the wisdom of the Egyptians. Yet, he remained with a disability.

Physical or learning disabilities can often make us feel that we are worth less than the next person. They can also be a real blow to our confidence, especially when it comes to being a tool of God. Throughout our education, we can be looked down on and called "special" or "slow". Physical disabilities can leave us sitting on the side and isolated watching everyone else have fun.

Did God make a mistake choosing a stuttering fugitive shepherd to lead his people out of captivity? Not a chance! While our weaknesses appear huge and debilitating to us, God sees past them to the perfect way he made us. In the very next verses following Moses admitting his weakness, God reminds Moses that He is the one who gave us mouths, the one who makes us with perfect weaknesses. Psalm 139:13-14 says, *"For you created my inmost being; you knit me together in my mother's womb. I praise you because I am fearfully and wonderfully made; your works are wonderful, I know that full well."* God created us wonderfully. He shaped us perfectly for the calling he has given us.

We all have weaknesses, but we must recognize that they are not a hindrance to God using our lives, but a benefit. After begging God to take away his weakness, Paul wrote in 2 Corinthians 12:9-10, *"But [God] said to me, 'My grace is sufficient for you, for my power is made perfect in weakness.' Therefore, I will boast all the more gladly about my weaknesses, so that Christ's power may rest on me. That is why, for Christ's sake, I delight in weaknesses, in insults, in hardships, in persecutions, in difficulties. For when I am weak, then I am strong."*

Do not waste your time listening to the Enemy or others who tell you that you are not good enough, bright enough, or strong enough for God to use. The question we should ask is, "Are we weak enough?" I personally always struggled with reading and writing in school, yet you are currently reading this devotional I wrote. God made us perfect. No physical, learning or mental disabilities disqualify you from His calling on your life. Do not resent your weakness, but boast in them so that Christ's power may rest on you.

Related Passages:

1. Psalm 139:13-14

2. 2 Corinthians 12:9-10

3. Exodus 3:17

4. Hebrews 11:23-28

Day 13
Simon the Zealot – God Sees Past Bad Associations

Key Passage: *"When morning came, [Jesus] called his disciples to him and chose twelve of them, whom he also designated apostles: Simon (whom he named Peter), his brother Andrew, James, John, Philip, Bartholomew, Matthew, Thomas, James son of Alphaeus, Simon who was called the Zealot, Judas son of James, and Judas Iscariot, who became a traitor."* Luke 6:13-16

Have you ever been in a group with someone who shares the same name as you? If so, you understand the confusion this can cause. Throughout my school years, I would often respond to a teacher to find that she was not speaking to me, but to another Jonathan. Similarly, Jesus had two disciples named 'Simon.' One features heavily in the Gospels and wrote two books of the New Testament. We commonly know him as Peter. All we know about the other Simon is that he is called the 'Zealot', and even that was probably a title only included by Luke to differentiate him from Simon Peter.

The Zealots were a group of rebel freedom fighters. Before Judea became a Roman province, the Israelites paid a 20% of their income to support the Levites, priests, and the temple. But when the Romans conquered Judea, they added an extra tax for Rome. Many historians believe the result was that the Israelites paid at least a 40% income tax. The Zealots decided to rebel from Rome and fight for Jewish freedom.

The first-century historian Josephus described them as 'sicarii,' a term that refers to people armed with daggers. Because of this, it is believed that the Zealots would often rely on terrorism to achieve their goals by concealing knives in their clothing and assassinating those regarded as enemies. Whether Simon himself had been physically involved in this rebellion or not, he was most definitely a supporter of them.

As such, Simon the Zealot was a radical and potentially a political and moral liability to Jesus. Yet, Jesus places him in his inner circle along with Matthew who was a tax collector for Rome and a potential mark for a Zealot assassination. Simon would have been watched by the authorities and all those who knew he was a Zealot. Jesus would have been judged by many as guilty by association. In fact, in Matthew 11:19 the people say, *"Here is a glutton and a drunkard, a friend of tax collectors and sinners."*

Maybe, like Simon, you have been involved with the wrong crowd or feel stuck in your social circle. You look at the people you associate with and conclude that God would never choose you. Whether you are in a gang you can't leave, a corrupt business group, a cult, or simply have friends who dishonour God, this is not the sum of your life.

When Jesus chose twelve men to be His disciples, He chose Simon the Zealot. Jesus knew who Simon was, including his past and his friends, but He also knew that Simon would respond to the call to leave both behind and follow Him. Jesus invites us all to leave our mistakes and enter into a close personal relationship with Him.

Related Passages:

1. Luke 6:13-16

2. Matthew 11:19

3. 1 Corinthians 15:33

4. Proverbs 12:26

5. Proverbs 18:24

Day 14
Zacchaeus - God Reforms Sinners

Key Passage: *"A man was there by the name of Zacchaeus; he was a chief tax collector and was wealthy. He wanted to see who Jesus was, but because he was short he could not see over the crowd. So he ran ahead and climbed a sycamore tree to see him, since Jesus was coming that way. When Jesus reached the spot, he looked up and said to him, 'Zacchaeus, come down immediately. I must stay at your house today.' So he came down at once and welcomed him gladly.*

All the people saw this and began to mutter, 'He has gone to be the guest of a sinner.' But Zacchaeus stood up and said to the Lord, 'Look, Lord! Here and now I give half of my possessions to the poor, and if I have cheated anybody out of anything, I will pay back four times the amount.' Jesus said to him, 'Today salvation has come to this house, because this man too is a son of Abraham. For the Son of Man came to seek and to save the lost.'" Luke 19:2-10

All of Zacchaeus' life he had been laughed at and rejected. We can imagine that throughout his childhood he was made fun of for being short. It must have been a great joy when he became a tax collector:

he could finally pay his peers back for all those bad comments and jokes.

Tax collectors worked for the Roman government. Most Jews considered them to be traitors. After all, their job was to take money from their own people to fund the enemy. The Romans made locals tax collectors and told them to collect a certain amount each quarter. Anything they made over this amount, they were free to keep for themselves. Consequently, extortion was commonplace as the tax collectors took all they could from the poor and the rich alike to fund the oppressor and their own lifestyle.

In becoming a tax collector, Zacchaeus improved his life. People still did not like him, gossiping about him behind his back, but now he had a measure of power in return. Then one day, Jesus came to his town. Zacchaeus saw a crowd had already gathered, but he wanted the chance to meet Jesus. It is likely that Zacchaeus heard of how Jesus had performed miracles, feeding large crowds of people. He had probably also heard the rumors of the strange holy man who touched the untouchables and ate with sinners. We do not really know exactly what hearsay had reached Zacchaeus, but we can discern how desperate he was to see Jesus.

Zacchaeus picked up his gown and ran to a tree. This was such a shameful thing for a middle-eastern man to do. The people in the crowd no doubt looked on in disbelief. They would have laughed and mocked him from a distance, but he did not care. I wonder if we show the same determination in coming to Jesus?

Zacchaeus was a little man, so like a child, he could have pushed himself through the crowd and to the front, but rather he climbs a tree. Maybe he was scared that a zealot in the crowd would stab him, but more likely, he wanted to meet Jesus but was too ashamed.

Zacchaeus' name means "pure one." It is the last name you would expect for a corrupt government official; Zacchaeus was anything but pure. Yet when Jesus stops at the tree where Zacchaeus is hiding, Jesus calls him by name. By calling Zacchaeus by name, Jesus was saying, "Pure one, I'm coming to your house today." Jesus was affirming what he saw in Zacchaeus, not what he was. While God does see our offensive sin, He also recognizes the transforming power of grace made available to us through Christ.

Maybe you feel afraid to draw near to Jesus because of the things you've done. Perhaps you are ashamed or even fearful of His judgement. God will one day judge the world for its sin, but Jesus also said in John 6:27 *"All those the Father gives me will come to me, and whoever comes to me I will never drive away."* Today is a day of grace and Jesus is inviting us to come to Him.

Can you imagine what Zacchaeus must have thought when Jesus called his name? Exultation that a prophet knew his name, but terrified that such a holy person might also know all of his sin and choose to hate him like everyone else. Jesus knows everything about us, but calls us anyway. Despite any trepidation he may have felt, Zacchaeus rushed down and went home with Jesus and in turn, Zacchaeus life was changed. As Jesus said, *"Today salvation has come to this house, because this man, too, is a son of Abraham."*[1] If your life is filled with rejection and you feel unable to come to Jesus, remember Zacchaeus. Salvation can also come to your house this day if only you welcome Jesus into your life.

Related Passages:

1. Luke 19:9

2. John 6:37

3. Romans 5:8-10

Day 15
Thomas – God Transforms Doubt to Faith

Key Passage: *"Now Thomas, one of the Twelve, was not with the disciples when Jesus came. So the other disciples told him, 'We have seen the Lord!' But he said to them, 'Unless I see the nail marks in his hands and put my finger where the nails were, and put my hand into his side, I will not believe.' A week later his disciples were in the house again, and Thomas was with them. Though the doors were locked, Jesus came and stood among them and said, 'Peace be with you!' Then he said to Thomas, 'Put your finger here; see my hands. Reach out your hand and put it into my side. Stop doubting and believe.' Thomas said to him, 'My Lord and my God!'"* John 20:24-28

Thomas was another of the Twelve disciples. His name means 'twin' and many historians believe that Matthew was his twin brother. However, Thomas is commonly remembered as "Doubting Thomas." This title has even become a phrase of everyday speech to describe a skeptic who refuses to believe in something.

Thomas was one of those people who needs to know the facts and figures before believing something. In our world, he would be one of the few individuals who read the small print before signing a document. He was someone who had to be sure before acting. However, singling him out as the doubter is a little unfair; the other disciples did not believe Mary and the other women either when they said they had seen Jesus alive.

Perhaps you can relate to this kind of mindset. Perhaps you're not a doubter, but you are prudent, possibly even over cautious at times. Do you tend to find yourself over analyzing the next action? Do you spend so much time thinking about doing something, that you actually miss the opportunity? Well, that was Thomas. When Jesus spoke about going to prepare a place for His people, John 14:5 says *"Thomas said to him, 'Lord, we don't know where you are going, so how can we know the way?'"* Thomas needed details to trust and believe.

The account which gave Thomas his nickname follows Jesus' resurrection. The women had met the angels at the tomb who told them that Jesus was alive. Peter and John had gone themselves and seen an empty tomb and grave clothes. That evening, Jesus had appeared to all the disciples, except Thomas who was not there.

We do not know why Thomas was not there, but we can imagine his shock and disbelief when the other disciples tell him that they had seen Jesus, alive. He responds not with rejoicing, but by saying:

"Unless I see the nail marks in his hands and put my finger where the nails were, and put my hand into his side, I will not believe."[1]

Thomas lived with his questions for one week, doubting the testimony of those closest to him and reexamining all the facts before Jesus appeared to him. Finally, Thomas had the proof that he needed; there was no more doubt. He makes the great confession, *"My Lord and my God!"*

In the Bible, these are the last recorded words spoken by Thomas. Church tradition says he took the gospel east, first to Babylon, and eventually on to India. Everywhere he went he proclaimed the message of the living Jesus. When Thomas found answers, he was a man who was willing to wholeheartedly embrace and act on them.

There are many who sit in church each week and wonder whether the message of the Bible can really be true. For some, it seems too wonderful to be real. We wonder whether God can really forgive sin, conquer death, and have an amazing plan for our little lives. Doubt and questions do not hinder you from being used by God. It's a myth that good Christians are free of doubt. The important thing is what we do with our insecurities. Thomas took them to Jesus, and Jesus went beyond giving Thomas answers; He gave Thomas Himself. Doubt does not cancel faith, but gives way to faith. If you are filled with questions today, take them to Jesus.

Related Passages:

1. John 20:25

2. John 14

3. John 20:1-24

4. James 1:5-8

Day 16
Jonah – God Forgives Disobedience

Key Passage: *"The word of the LORD came to Jonah son of Amittai: 'Go to the great city of Nineveh and preach against it, because its wickedness has come up before me.' But Jonah ran away from the LORD and headed for Tarshish. He went down to Joppa, where he found a ship bound for that port. After paying the fare, he went aboard and sailed for Tarshish to flee from the LORD."* Jonah 1:1-3

Often in life, we struggle to know what to do next. How many times have you sought God for guidance over a decision? Maybe you are choosing a college or a new job. Perhaps you are contemplating a relationship or a missionary calling. There are many times we are uncertain of what God really wants us to do, but Jonah did not have this problem. The book of Jonah begins with God directly telling Jonah what to do next.

Nineveh was a great city, but they were also the enemies of Jonah's people, the Israelites. When God told Jonah that in a little over a month Nineveh was going to be destroyed, this would have been the best news Jonah had heard in a long time! It would have been like a village in WWII, oppressed by Nazi rule, receiving the news that in forty days the Nazis would be no more. Imagine the rejoicing! There would finally be freedom from the enemy, and their oppressors would receive the punishment they deserved.

This was great news for Jonah, except he understood God is *"gracious and compassionate God, slow to anger and abounding in love, a God who relents from sending calamity."*[2] God is full of compassion but Jonah was not. He wanted the people who had hurt the Israelites to suffer and be destroyed. Jonah cared nothing for the *"hundred and twenty thousand people who cannot tell their right hand from their left—and also many animals?"*[3] He cared nothing for the babies and children of this sinful city. In Jonah's eyes, they deserved all the punishment they got.

Jonah hated them so much he would rather run from God and suffer punishment himself than give them a chance to repent. Jonah's disobedience was not gradual or by mistake. It was cold, calculated, wilful disobedience. He knew what God wanted, but it was not what he wanted.

So Jonah ran in the opposite direction, and we know the account well. There is a storm and he is thrown overboard only to be eaten by a big fish. He remains there for three days. When he cries out in repentance, God gives him a second chance and Jonah travels to

Nineveh. He preaches and revival breaks out; the whole city turns to God in repentance.

Every single preacher I know would be overjoyed if an entire city of 120,000 repented when they preached. Not Jonah. In Jonah 4:19, Jonah sits on the hilltop and says to God: *"I'm so angry I wish I were dead."* Jonah appreciated it when God gave him a second chance, but he hated the fact that God gave his enemies a second chance too. The last words in the book of Jonah are a rebuke to Jonah from God: *"But the LORD said, '...should I not have concern for the great city of Nineveh, in which there are more than a hundred and twenty thousand people who cannot tell their right hand from their left—and also many animals?'"*[3]

The book of Jonah ends right there. We don't know what happens to Jonah. Does he repent, or does he stay angry at God? Does he learn from his lesson? It seems a bad place to stop, but it's a reminder that the book of Jonah was never about Jonah. It is about God and his compassion. God was showing how much He loves people and how much compassion He has towards us.

God can use us even if we are reluctant. Jonah missed out on the blessing of being used by God. He missed the joy of seeing people turn from their sins to God in repentance because of his reluctance, prejudice and hatred. Is there something that is causing you to lose out on the joy of being used by God? Surrender it to

God today and ask him to change your heart.

Related Passages:

1. Jonah 3:4

2. Jonah 4:2

3. Jonah 4:10-11

Day 17
John Mark – God Allows Second Chances

Key Passage: *"Do your best to come to me quickly, for Demas, because he loved this world, has deserted me and has gone to Thessalonica. Crescens has gone to Galatia, and Titus to Dalmatia. Only Luke is with me. Get Mark and bring him with you, because he is helpful to me in my ministry."* 2 Timothy 4:9-11

There are few things worse than being let down by a close friend when you need them the most. John Mark was brought up in a house of prayer. In Acts 12:12, we read that after Peter was miraculously rescued from prison *"he went to the house of Mary the mother of John, also called Mark, where many people had gathered and were praying."* As a young man, he was surrounded by the men who God used to create the New Testament church. He would have grown up getting to know the real men away from the public, listening to their stories of their time with Jesus, and hearing their struggles and prayer requests.

As a child, I can imagine John Mark dreaming that He too would be able to fulfill the great commission, traveling throughout the world and preaching the gospel. His uncle was Barnabas, so when Paul and Barnabas were appointed to go on their missionary journey, John Mark's opportunity arrived. Acts 13:5 says, *"When they arrived at Salamis, they proclaimed the word of God in the Jewish synagogues. John was with them as their helper."* He was given the job of working behind the scenes, taking care of the details so Paul and Barnabas could focus on ministry. What a privilege! Most of us would jump at the chance to be at the cutting edge of what God is doing in world missions.

But something happened. Eight verses later we read in Acts 13:13, *"From Paphos, Paul and his companions sailed to Perga in Pamphylia, where John left them to return to Jerusalem."* The Greek word translated as 'left,' actually is closer in meaning to 'desert'. In other words, John Mark willfully abandoned Paul and Barnabas. We do not know why he left. It is possible he was homesick. Maybe he missed having servants, preferring to be served than to serve. Perhaps he faced the problem that many young missionaries, church planters, and pastors face: unrealistic expectations of miracles and revival at every moment. Instead, he was setting up chairs, waiting around, and otherwise taking care of normal everyday details.

Whatever the reason, when Barnabas wanted to take him on their next journey, Paul thought John Mark had messed up too badly and was not prepared to give him a second chance. Maybe you have made mistakes that have left enduring limitations in your life. John Mark probably thought he had missed his chance and it was all over, especially when Paul rejected him for a second missions trip. Well in Paul's view it was, but in Barnabas' and God's view, there is always a second chance.

In the years that follow, John Mark proves himself over and over again. Paul forgives him and even goes on to request John Mark when he needs help. If John Mark had ever wondered if he would get another chance to fulfill his calling and be involved in ministry, it must have been wonderful confirmation to have Paul change his mind and decide he was valuable. From John Mark's life, we can be encouraged that failure in ministry does not erase the potential of God using you in the future. People may give up on us, but God never will.

John Mark is also the author of the gospel of Mark: the most translated book of the Bible in all the world. What a turnaround for a man who gave up on his first missions trip! All of us have failed, but by God's strength, we can get back up and keep serving.

Related Passages:

1. Acts 13:5-13

2. Acts 15:37-39

3. Corinthians 4:10

4. Colossians 4:10

5. 2 Timothy 4:9-11

Day 18
Aaron – God Maintains the Easily Influenced

Key Passage: *"And no one takes this honor on himself, but he receives it when called by God, just as Aaron was."* Hebrews 5:4

Aaron was Moses' older brother. He was born in a slave hut in Egypt, just old enough to miss the Pharaoh's order to kill all baby boys at birth which affected Moses. Nevertheless, he was born into a time and place where the only future for him was slavery.

Aaron and Moses probably had a broken relationship growing up. While Moses was living as a prince of Egypt, enjoying the best of everything Egypt had to offer, Aaron was making bricks in the hot desert sun. While Moses attended banquets at the palace, Aaron lived on sparse rations. While Moses slept in a comfortable bed with servants to attend him, Aaron lived with other families in a squalid slum. They lived worlds apart.

As Aaron approached eighty-three years old, God lays it on his heart to visit his younger brother who was currently a fugitive in the wilderness. Little did

Aaron know that God had spoken to Moses through a burning bush and appointed Aaron to be his mouthpiece.

After being used to deliver the people from Egypt, Aaron rose to became the first high priest of God's people. There was no higher position among the people of Israel. Aaron was responsible for teaching the people how to honor God in all aspects of life. People came to him to make offerings for their sins and he could even enter the Most Holy Place in the tabernacle.

Aaron had the most important job on earth, but he was still a man. Consequently, like us, he had failures and weaknesses. In Aaron's case, he was a people pleaser, easily lead, who did not like to say no. We can sympathize, because we too often struggle to say no to things we know are wrong rather than risk upsetting or offending someone. Too often, we are guided by other people's opinions, thoughts, criticisms, and approval. Typically, the need to always please others is deeply rooted in either a fear of rejection or failure.

Left alone for forty days as Moses went up Mount Sinai, Aaron couldn't cope with the pressure of leading the people. Exodus 32:1 says *"When the people saw that Moses was so long in coming down from the mountain, they gathered around Aaron and said, "Come, make us gods who will go before us. As for this fellow Moses who brought us up out of Egypt, we don't know what has happened to him."* Aaron should have rebuked them and refused their request, but he feared their rejection and made a golden calf for them to worship.

Aaron had a similar problem at home. All parents know what it is like to give in to your children instead of disciplining them the way we ought. We sometimes go against our better judgement because we just want them to be happy. Aaron's two sons did not take the calling to serve as priests seriously, and as a result they were killed by God. Aaron was not even allowed to mourn for them. To make matters worse, his access into God's presence was restricted.

Aaron was also easily influenced by his sister Miriam. He joined her in gossip and disrespecting Moses for marrying a Cushite woman.[1] Once again he was carried along by others to do what he knew was wrong.

We too must guard ourselves against people pleasing. Paul wrote in Galatians 1:10 *"Am I now trying to win the approval of human beings, or of God? Or am I trying to please people? If I were still trying to please people, I would not be a servant of Christ."* Paul is reminding us that while we are called to love others, we must always love God in first and seek to please Him above everyone else.

Related Passages:

1. Numbers 12

2. Leviticus 10:1

3. Leviticus 16:1-2

4. Exodus 32:4

Day 19
Miriam – God Humbles the Proud

Key Passage: *"Miriam and Aaron began to talk against Moses because of his Cushite wife, for he had married a Cushite. 'Has the Lord spoken only through Moses?' they asked. 'Hasn't he also spoken through us? And the Lord heard this ."* Numbers 12:1-2

Miriam is introduced to us as a protective sister and obedient daughter. When Moses was placed in the basket on the river Nile, it was Miriam's job to stand at a distance watching to ensure he was okay. Even at a young age, we see her courage and quick thinking. When Pharaoh's daughter has compassion on Moses, Miriam, a little slave girl, is brave enough to speak to the princess of Egypt and arranged a deal whereby Moses did not only live, but her mother got paid to look after him. We can only imagine how excited Miriam must have been to tell her mother what she had done.

The next time we meet Miriam, she is leading the people in worship. After crossing the dead sea on dry land and being delivered from the Egyptian army, Exodus 15:20-21 says, *"Then Miriam the prophet,*

Aaron's sister, took a timbrel in her hand, and all the women followed her, with timbrels and dancing. Miriam sang to them: 'Sing to the LORD, for he is highly exalted. Both horse and driver he has hurled into the sea.'" In Micah, Miriam is called a prophetess, which means God used Miriam to reveal Himself and will to his people. Miriam, along with her brothers, was in the middle of everything God was doing and was instrumental in leading the people.

Over time, however, Miriam changed from being Moses' supportive sister to his rival. Maybe she did not agree with some of the decisions he made and thought Aaron could have done a better job. Perhaps, the way the other women looked up to her went to her head, and she started to think too much of herself. Possibly, it was an age thing. After all, she was the older sister who had saved Moses life. In all likelihood, it was a gradual change of heart caused by a combination of all these things.

It all comes to a head in Numbers 12 after Moses married a Cushite woman. It could have been a racial issue, as Moses wife was not Jewish, or it could be that Miriam saw her as a rival to her position. Either way, she starts to speak against Moses and question his position as leader of the Israelites. Miriam, despite being called to be a prophetess in her own right, wanted to be equal with God's appointed leader. She tried to promote herself and as a result, God gave her leprosy. She was sent outside of the camp alone for seven days. Can you imagine what went through her mind while there? She was probably embarrassed and humbled but eventually brought to a place of repentance.

Miriam was very influential and given a position of leadership by God. Consequently, she was held accountable by God for misusing that influence and position for her own gain. Do you sometimes try to use your prestige for personal benefit? Paul writes in Romans 12:3, *"For by the grace given me I say to every one of you: Do not think of yourself more highly than you ought, but rather think of yourself with sober judgment, in accordance with the faith God has distributed to each of you."*

Are you satisfied with the position God has given you? Do you often look down on people God has appointed to shepherd you, thinking you could do a better job? Do you verbalize this to undermine them? Miriam is a warning to be thankful for what God has given us, waiting patiently should He choose to provide us with further authority. We ought to be careful to see ourselves in light of God's Word, not public opinion, past experiences, and certainly not through the eyes of our own ego!

Related Passages:

1. Exodus 2

2. Micah 6:4

3. Numbers 12:1-10

Day 20
The Boy with a Packed Lunch – God Multiplies Little

Key Passage: *"Here is a boy with five small barley loaves and two small fish, but how far will they go among so many?"* John 6:9

It can be easy to compare ourselves to others. Often, we wish we had as much to give as others. Maybe you have desired a better voice so you could help with worship or better public speaking skills so you could share the gospel with confidence. Perhaps you have seen a local food drive and wanted to donate, but struggle to feed your family.

We do not know much about the boy mentioned in John, not even his name. We do not know if he was on the hillside alone, with family, or with friends. We do not know how old he was. What we do know is that he was in the right place at the right time. By God's providence, he was willing to give all that he had to Jesus.

I can imagine a young boy begging his parents for permission to go and listen to Jesus. The whole country was telling stories of Jesus and his miracles, and I can see this little boy wanting to hear Jesus for himself, even at a distance. A celebrity had come to town, like when people gather today to see the Queen, President or Pope.

I can envision his mother packing him a lunch with instructions not to be home too late and to stay out of trouble. When he arrived, there was a huge crowd: 5,000 men, plus women and children. Being small, he probably pushed himself to the front so he could see a miracle for himself. As he listens to Jesus teach the hours feel like minutes, and he does not even realized he has forgotten to eat his lunch.

When he overhears Jesus speaking to his disciples about food, he remembers he still has his packed lunch of five small barley loaves and two small fish. At that time, barley bread was the cheapest of all bread, and the fish were only small. He did not have much to offer to Jesus, but in an act of selflessness, he decides to give it all away. I suppose he thought at least that way Jesus would not be hungry.

Jesus prayed and fed the entire crowd of 5000 men, plus the uncounted women and children, because of one little boy's generous heart. Amazingly, the boy himself also received more bread and fish than he started with and ate well. The Bible tells us there were twelve baskets of leftovers after everyone had finished eating.

Like the young boy, God wants us to bring what we have to Him. The quantity or the quality is not as important as the heart in which we give it. 2 Corinthians 9:7 says *"Each of you should give what you have decided in your heart to give, not reluctantly or under compulsion, for God loves a cheerful giver."* Furthermore, what we bring is not as important as to whom we bring it. The boy gave his lunch to Jesus, and He multiplied it to feed the multitude. God is not interested in the gifts we do not have. As we offer sacrifices to God, he wants to bless all that we do have. Regardless of how little or insignificant our gifts may appear in our own eyes, God sees their potential. Even if you do not feel like you have much to offer God, hand it over to Jesus and watch him multiply it.

Related Passages:

1. 2 Corinthians 9:7

2. Luke 21:1-4

3. 1 Kings 17:7-16

Day 21
Naomi – God Recalls the Wanderer

Key Passage: *"I went away full, but the LORD has brought me back empty. Why call me Naomi? The LORD has afflicted me; the Almighty has brought misfortune upon me."* Ruth 1:21

In Scripture, Moab represents a place of worldly compromise. While other nations attacked Israel while they were wandering in the desert, the Moabites offered a hand of friendship. They invited them to join their societies, worship their gods, and marry their women: everything God had told them not to do. This tactic was far more sinister than a straightforward military attack. It made them lower their guard and compromise their beliefs for short term pleasures.

When we meet Naomi, she is a widow and a foreigner in Moab. Naomi had moved there just for a 'while' with her husband and sons because there was a famine in Israel.[1] However, that 'while' became years. Naomi and her family settled down and her sons married Moabite women. Not long after, the place that looked so inviting becomes a place of devastation: Naomi's husband and two sons die. I wonder how many people have gotten into inviting relationships they knew were wrong only for them to end in distress. How many people have taken a new job which promised the world, but brought misery? How many people have moved into a new house for a better life, but became bankrupt? We understand the situation Naomi was in because we too often find ourselves there.

Naomi looked at her future and saw only one outcome. If she stayed in Moab, she would end up dead like the rest of her family. So she decides it is time to turn around and return to the place of blessing. Is this not a picture of what repentance is? We find ourselves in the wrong place, so we make a U-turn, leaving the world behind and fixing our eyes on Jesus.

Naomi was out of touch with God and far away from his people, but she is determined to return to the place of blessing. So, she returns to Bethlehem with nothing except her daughter-in-law, Ruth, who refused to leave her. In Ruth 1:21 Naomi says, *"I went away full, but the LORD has brought me back empty. Why call me Naomi? The LORD has afflicted me; the Almighty has brought misfortune upon me."* She was poor and hungry, but at least she is now in the right place. Naomi's future was changed when she left the place of compromise and returned to God.

Have you allowed yourself to slowly drift into the world, living by its standards rather than God's laws?

Has it suddenly dawned upon you that you are spiritually wandering? If you find yourself in the wrong place today, whether it be physical, mental or spiritual, it is time to return to God. Acts 3:19 says *"Repent, then, and turn to God, so that your sins may be wiped out, that times of refreshing may come from the Lord."* Do you need a time of refreshing? Turn to God! If our decisions have led you further and further away from God, it is not too late. Turn to God!

Naomi had lost her sons in Moab, but listen to what the women told her in Ruth 4:14-15, *"Praise be to the LORD, who this day has not left you without a guardian-redeemer. May he become famous throughout Israel! He will renew your life and sustain you in your old age. For your daughter-in-law, who loves you and who is better to you than seven sons, has given him birth."* With Naomi's return to Israel, God gives Naomi a daughter-in-law who loves her more than seven sons and a grandson who will became King David's grandfather. God restores to Naomi more than she had lost, but it all began with her returning to the right place.

Related Passages:

1. Ruth 1:1

2. Matthew 1

3. Ruth 1-4

Day 22
Onesimus: God Captures the Runaway Slave

Key Passage: *"I appeal to you for my son Onesimus, who became my son while I was in chains. Formerly he was useless to you, but now he has become useful both to you and to me."* Philemon 1:10-11

Onesimus was a runaway slave. Paul wrote to his master, Philemon, who was also a Christian. Even from this short letter, we can see Philemon was generous, caring, prayerful, and kind. We can but imagine Philemon's pain when he learned that Onesimus had not only ran away but also robbed him. As his neighbors heard of Onesimus' action, they would have questioned the way Philmon had treated him. As such, his name and testimony would have been questioned. Our actions always affect other, either directly or indirectly.

Under Roman law, there were no limits to the punishment a master could inflict on his runaway slave. If the slave was caught, the master could choose to have the slave returned to them or put to death. This was sentence hanging over Onesimus' head when he ran away with his master's possessions.

Onesimus ran off to Rome. His goal was to hide away in the big city, something we can easily understand. How often do we run away from our problems or try to hide our mistakes and failings?

Rome seemed a safe choice for Onesimus, but despite his best efforts, he was arrested. Not by the Romans, but by the Gospel of Jesus Christ. Onesimus was experiencing the same lesson as Jonah; you can't outrun God. In the large city of Rome, God sought a runaway slave hiding from the punishment he deserved and touched him with grace. What a reminder of God's love for sinners! Where did God find you? He has shown great love for each of us, that while we were running from him and living in a life of sin, he sought us and called us.

Onesimus is transformed by salvation. Paul calls him in Colossians 4:9, *"a faithful and dear brother"*. As we read at the beginning, Paul becomes so close to Onesimus that he feels like Onesimus has become his son. No longer a useless runaway, the slave has become a son and a friend. What a picture of what has happened to each of us in Christ! Jesus said in John 15:15, *"I no longer call you servants, because a servant does not know his master's business. Instead, I have called you friends, for everything that I learned from my Father I have made known to you."*

Onesimus life was changed. God had forgiven him, but the punishment of being a runaway slave still hung over him. Maybe you have repented of your sin to God, but still avoid the people you have wronged. You have responded to the gospel, but have not resolved the consequences of your past mistakes. Paul tells Onesimus that as a Christian he should go back to Philemon and put things right. It was time to seek forgiveness from Philmon for the wrong that he had caused, so Onesimus could be free of his past actions to be used where God wanted.

Paul aids his return by writing a letter to Philemon, asking that Philemon will receive Onesimus *"no longer as a slave, but better than a slave, as a dear brother."*[1] Furthermore, Paul says that he will repay any debt Philemon feels Onesimus owes. What a glorious picture of what Christ has done for us!

Are you running away from something you need to put right? Have you given up on being used by God simply to focus on avoiding punishment? Remember Onesimus, and face your past. God loves you so much, he sought you out and is calling you to become a dear child, useful to Himself and others.

Related Passages:

1. Philemon 1:16

2. Colossians 4:9

3. Philemon 1:1-25

Day 23
David – God Forgives
Moments of Failure

Key Passage: *"After removing Saul, [God] made David their king. God testified concerning him: 'I have found David son of Jesse, a man after my own heart; he will do everything I want him to do.'"* Acts 13:22

King David is one of the most significant figures in the Old Testament and Jewish history. He is named in 1 Samuel, 2 Samuel, 1 Kings, 1 Chronicles, and wrote seventy-five psalms! In 1 Samuel we meet David, the youngest son, forgotten about while looking after sheep in the field. While Samuel and David's own father were looking for someone who looked like a king, *"The LORD said to Samuel, "Do not consider his appearance or his height, for I have rejected him. The LORD does not look at the things people look at. People look at the outward appearance, but the LORD looks at the heart."*[1] David is presented to us as someone who has the right heart for God to use.

David moves on to become a musician for King Saul. By the next chapter, still not old enough to join the army, he has killed the giant Goliath and chased off the Philistine army. David became a great military leader, so successful that King Saul gives him a high rank in the army, which pleases all the troops, and Saul's officers as well.

Saul becomes jealous of David and tries to kill him time after time. On more than one occasion, David is given a chance to kill Saul, but refuses as Saul is the Lord's anointed king of the LORD. I doubt many of us would have reacted the same to someone who was trying to kill us.

David eventually becomes King. God said concerning him: *'I have found a man after my own heart; who will do everything I want him to do.'"* David was a great man used powerfully by God. He was a humble and submissive to authority. He was a great shepherd caring for others. Nevertheless, whenever we speak of David, we are also reminded of Bathsheba.

From his bedroom window, David catches a glimpse of Bathsheba, the wife Uriah the Hittite, bathing on the roof. David is overcome by lust, sleeps with her, and she becomes pregnant. David sets out on a plan to cover up his sin. First, he summons Uriah from his posting in the army to try and get him to sleep with his wife. However, Uriah refuses to go home while his men are in battle. Next, David tries to get Uriah drunk to change his mind, but again this fails. Running out of options, David sends him back to the army with instructions to his general to ensure Uriah is killed. This was nothing less than murder.

What a turnaround! David's downward spiral took him from a man who refused to kill King Saul, even though Saul was trying to kill him, to a man who kills to cover up his own sin. We would think this unforgivable; it would be the end for David. Could anyone fall any lower?

Here we again see God's grace to us. God sends Nathan, a prophet, to speak to David about his sin. David responds with repentance. 2 Samuel 12:13 says, *"Then David said to Nathan, "I have sinned against the LORD." Nathan replied, "The LORD has taken away your sin. You are not going to die."*

How we deal with our sin has a direct influence on how God can use us. We can either try to cover our sins while drifting further and further away from God, or we can turn in repentance to God. After all, He is faithful and just and will forgive us our sins and purify us from all unrighteousness. If you are backsliding today, God is graciously giving you the chance to turn to him in repentance. Please embrace this day of grace.

Related Passages:

1. 1 Samuel 16:7-11

2. 1 Samuel 18:5

3. 1 Samuel 24:6

4. 2 Samuel 11:1

5. 2 Samuel 12:13

6. 1 John 1:9

Day 24
John the Baptist – God Anoints a Messenger

Key Passage: *"In those days John the Baptist came to the Judean wilderness and began preaching. His message was, 'Repent of your sins and turn to God, for the Kingdom of Heaven is near.'"* Matthew 3:1-2

John the Baptist was Jesus' cousin. Like Jesus, his birth was foretold by an angel, and he was named before his birth. We read in Luke 1:5 that both his parents were descendants of Aaron. This means that John's future was already planned out for him. Like everyone following in the line of Aaron, including his father, he would be expected to become a priest of Israel.

If John had followed in his family business, he would have been honored by the people and financially comfortable. Yet this was not John's calling. As the angel Gabriel spoke in Luke 1:17, *"And [John] will go on before the Lord, in the spirit and power of Elijah, to turn the hearts of the parents to their children and the disobedient to the wisdom of the righteous—to make ready a people prepared for the Lord."* John's calling was not that of a priest but of a prophet like Elijah. Consequently, he turns his back on the comfort he could have and sets out for the wilderness to prepare the way for the Lord.

Throughout church history, there have been many who were called to leave comfortable lives behind to follow God's calling. When Jesus called the first disciples to follow Him, they left everything behind. Many a missionary has left the comforts of home to travel to distant lands and preach the gospel. I wonder if we would respond in the same way if called. Are we willing to leave the comforts of our homes for the sake of Christ? God does not always ask us to travel to a distant land; it could be helping out in a soup kitchen or the children's ministry at your church. Are you willing to leave your comfort zone for Jesus?

John's message was simple: *"Repent, for the kingdom of heaven has come near."*[1] It was not a popular message with the religious leaders of the day, but it was the message the people needed to hear. Interestingly, John did not preach repentance throughout a city like Jonah. Even though John was alone in the wilderness, people went to him because they recognized the power of God in the message he proclaimed. Historians believe that more than a million-people travelled out into the wilderness to hear John preach.

Often in our witnessing, we do not understand the power of the gospel. We think we need to come up with compelling arguments with advanced apologetics before we share the gospel. While there is a place for these things, they don't affect the power of the gospel message. Paul wrote in Romans 1:16, "*For I am not ashamed of the gospel because it is the power of God that brings salvation to everyone who believes: first to the Jew, then to the Gentile.*" John's message was simple, but it was anointed. We should have the same confidence in the message God has given us to proclaim.

John did not fit the mold of a respectable member of society. He wore clothes made of camel's hair, held up by a leather belt around his waist. His diet consisted of insects and wild honey. John was also a Nazarite, which means he never shaved or cut his hair. John was one scruffy preacher! Here again, we are reminded that it is not about the man, but the message. Despite his appearance, millions of people went to the wilderness where John was to hear his message and be baptized. What an impact!

John also recognized that it was not about him or his ministry. His job was to prepare the way for the Lord. John's whole life and ministry pointed people to Jesus. As John summed up his role in John 3:30, "[*Jesus] must become greater; I must become less.*" The first step of being used powerfully by God is recognizing that it is all about His glory and not our own. Our motivation for being used by God should never be for self, but to bring Him praise. Leave your insecurities about worthiness behind and concentrate on what God wants you to do.

Related Passages:

1. Matthew 3:1-7

2. Luke 1:5-17

3. Matthew 11:11

Day 25
Peter - God Works with the Impulsive

Key Passage: *"Immediately the cock crowed the second time. Then Peter remembered the word Jesus had spoken to him: 'Before the cock crows twice you will disown me three times.' And he broke down and wept."* Mark 14:72

Scripture records for us a very transparent picture of Peter's life. He was a man marked by impulsive actions, but also a man with great moments of faith. For example, in Matthew 4:18-20, we read that when Jesus called Peter and his brother Andrew to follow him, they left their nets immediately to follow him. During the stormy sea in Matthew 14:28, Peter says to Jesus *"'Lord, if it's you,' Peter replied, 'tell me to come to you on the water." "Come,' he said. Then Peter got down out of the boat, walked on the water and came toward Jesus."* In Matthew 16:16 when Jesus asked His disciples who they think he is, Peter immediately replies that he is the Messiah, the Son of the living God. Yet within a few verses of this confession and being called blessed by Jesus, we find Peter rebuking Jesus. Jesus turns and says to him in Matthew 16:23, *"Get behind me, Satan! You are a stumbling block to me; you do not have in mind the concerns of God, but merely human concerns."* What a difference a few verses can make!

These moments resemble our own life. We spend precious moments in God's presence during our devotional time and hear him speak to us through His Word. Yet, within moments of leaving the house, we find ourselves cursing a bad driver who cuts us off in traffic. We sit through an amazing church service, but when it is finished we start gossiping with the person sitting next to us. We, like Peter, change so quickly.

This is highlighted again in Peter's denial of Jesus. In Matthew 26:33 Peter says, *"Even if all fall away on account of you, I never will."* Yet, a mere 40 verses later, he has disowned Jesus three times. How often we also break our promises to God! We truthfully intend to keep our word at one moment and break it in the next. We find ourselves bartering with God, promising to do something in return for a favor. Perhaps in response to a conviction, we promise to cease a sin, or start a new good habit. So quickly we forget our promises and go back on our word.

Jesus graciously restores Peter and gives him the chance to declare his love as many time as he denied knowing Jesus. When Jesus returns to Heaven, and the Holy Spirit comes upon the church, we can already see a change in Peter. On the very day, he receives the Holy Spirit, Peter preaches and expounds on the Old Testament and three thousand people accepted the message and are baptized. In the days that follow, people recognize him as someone who has been with Jesus. In Acts 5:14-15 we read, *"more and more men and women believed in the Lord and were added to their number. As a result, people brought the sick into the streets and laid them on beds and mats so that at least Peter's shadow might fall on some of them as he passed by."*

Peter continued throughout his life to be changed by God. God continued to shape his understanding and use him powerfully. Peter continued to make mistakes, but God sustained him. What an incredible comfort for us, that God will continue to shape us and mold us into Christ image, even when we fail him! In 2 Corinthians 3:18 assures us that, like Peter, *"we all, who with unveiled faces contemplate the Lord's glory, are being transformed into his image with ever-increasing glory, which comes from the Lord, who is the Spirit."*

Related Passages:

1. Ecclesiastes 5:5

2. John 21

3. Acts 2:41

4. Acts 4:13

Day 26
Hosea – God Takes on a
Broken Family

Key Passage: *"The LORD said to me, "Go, show your love to your wife again, though she is loved by another man and is an adulteress. Love her as the LORD loves the Israelites, though they turn to other gods and love the sacred raisin cakes."* Hosea 3:1

Many a person has called out to God in prayer about a relationship. Who should I date? Is this the right person to marry? It is one the most important decisions we will ever make in life. Consequently, godly men and women do not make this decision rashly, but seek God's confirmation through prayer. If you're single today, the first question you should be asking is if it is God's will for you to marry at all. After receiving confirmation, pray that God will shape you into a good husband or wife and help your future spouse to grow into a stronger Christian.

Hosea was a young man called to preach by God. He lived in a time where the Israelite people had fallen away in sin. One of the first recorded things God says to him is rather shocking. Hosea 1:2 says, *"When the LORD began to speak through Hosea, the LORD said to him, 'Go, marry a promiscuous woman and have children with her, for like an adulterous wife this land is guilty of unfaithfulness to the LORD.'"* This is most certainly not the answer we would want in regards to our future spouse! Imagine a young man, just out of seminary, and called to preach. He is asking God for direction, and he receives a message to find a prostitute on the street and marry her. For Hosea, this was not *Pretty Woman*, this was his real life.

Hosea marries a prostitute named Gomer. Her name means "completion," and possibly for a few moments after getting married, he feels complete. Maybe when she marries Hosea, she promises to leave her sinful way of life behind to build a new life with her love. They begin a family together with a son, then a daughter, then another son. God tells Hosea to name his first son Jezreel, because the house of Jehu will be punished for the massacre at Jezreel. His only daughter he names Lo-Ruhamah, which means "not loved", for God will no longer show love to Israel. His youngest song is called Lo-Ammi, which means "not my people", for God declares the Israelites are no longer his people.

If you think your family life is messed up, think of Hosea. He is married to a prostitute, and his children are called massacre, unloved and not my people. The circumstances Hosea found himself in were as unique as God using his family life as an example of God's relationship with Israel. Nevertheless, there are many people who find themselves in complicated families. Maybe you or your spouse has been unfaithful, and you are trying to make it work, but the trust has gone. Maybe your children have run away from home. Perhaps you have brought them up in the church, but now they are an atheist, an addict, or in a sinful relationship. Whatever your circumstances, if you are living with a broken family, then you understand something of Hosea's pain. Consequently, you also grasp a portion of God's pain when people turn from Him and refuse His love.

Though your pain, God is giving you an understanding of how much He loves people. We can let this break us or motivate us to proclaim His love to a hurting world. The book of Hosea is a demonstration of God's love. When Hosea's wife runs off with another man, he buys her back: a foreshadowing of how Jesus would die to pay the price for our sins 400 years after Hosea. God's love is absolute. It's a love that rivers could not sweep away. God's love is unconditional, unconquerable and incomparable. He is the Father of the prodigal who runs out to hug the rebellious son, who wished him dead, and welcomes him back into the family.

If you have pain in your family, you understand that sin is not about breaking rules, but breaking hearts. When we sin, God's heart breaks because He wants the best for us, and that is never the sinful path. As God used Hosea's family as an example for the nation,

He can also use your pain as an example of his love for this world.

Related Passages:

1. Hosea 1:4-9

2. Song of Songs 8:7

3. Luke 15:11-32

Day 27
The Samaritan Woman –
God Breaks Sinful Patterns

Key Passage: *"So he came to a town in Samaria called Sychar, near the plot of ground Jacob had given to his son Joseph. Jacob's well was there, and Jesus, tired as he was from the journey, sat down by the well. It was about noon. When a Samaritan woman came to draw water, Jesus said to her, 'Will you give me a drink?'"* John 4:5-7

Have you ever been looked down on by others? Maybe you have made decisions you are ashamed of and, as a result, try to avoid people rather than experience their disapproving looks and words. It is one thing to deal with shame inside yourself, but it is quite another to deal with the harsh judgement of others.

In John 4 we meet a woman who was in this exact situation. Why else would you go out in the midday sun to collect water? Sensible people went out in the early morning while it was still cool and rested in the shade during the hottest hours. Knowing this, she made the most of the opportunity to get water from the well without having to bump into anyone.

We can imagine her disappointment when she arrives at the well and there is a man there. Worse than that, he was a Jew. The Jewish people looked down even on the best of the Samaritans. She likely kept her head down and tried to avoid any eye contact, both annoyed and surprised when the man asked her for a drink. She did not want to see anyone, and now this Jewish man was trying to start a conversation with her! Little did she know this man was Jesus.

Jesus starts discussing physical thirst but quickly moves on to spiritual thirst. Like many others, this lady thirsted to be loved. We can imagine her excitement on her first wedding day, followed by her disappointment when the joy shattered and the relationship she longed for brought her pain. She begins to long for freedom from marriage and consequently, she gets divorced. Then she gets lonely, and soon falls in love with another man. This time she is certain it will work, but yet again it fails. Her life continues in a circuit of loneliness, marriage, and divorce.

I wonder how often we find ourselves in repeating circle of pain over and over again? It may not be a relationship but something else, like dieting. You work hard to lose weight just to gain it all back plus more inches. For others, it is their savings. They struggle for prosperity but keep falling back into debt. How about your relationship with Christ? Maybe you keep backsliding. One moment, you're going to every service the church offers, reading your Bible and praying every day, but you continue to let yourself drift back into the world. We all have this pattern in our lives to some extent.

Jesus speaks to the woman and explains that her real thirst is not for a physical relationship but a spiritual relationship. For her, it was like continually drinking salt water: each sip only increased her thirst. The woman wanted to make sure she understood what Jesus was saying. In John 4:25, *"The woman said, 'I know that Messiah' (called Christ) 'is coming. When he comes, he will explain everything to us.'"* She is ready now for the final revelation of Christ to her soul. Jesus replies, *"I, the one speaking to you – I am he."* There was no more doubt. She had met her savior.

What effect did meeting Jesus have on this woman? John tells us that she was so excited that she forgot her water jar by the well and rushed back into town. The outcast is so energized that she voluntarily talks to people, telling them she has met the Messiah[1]. " Furthermore, many of the Samaritans from that town believed in Jesus because of the woman's testimony. The villagers go out to the well and invite Jesus to stay with them, and many more become believers during his stay. [2]

Jesus transformed this woman from someone who was ashamed to meet her neighbors on the street into a powerful evangelist telling everyone what Jesus had done in her life. Jesus transforms someone who had gone from one broken relationship to the next into someone who taught others how to restore a relationship with God. Oh, what wonder is the transforming power of God's grace!

Related Passages:

1. John 4:28-30

2. John 4:39-41

Day 28
Jabez – God Overcomes Pain

Key Passage: *"Jabez was more honorable than his brothers. His mother had named him Jabez, saying, 'I gave birth to him in pain.' Jabez cried out to the God of Israel, 'Oh, that you would bless me and enlarge my territory! Let your hand be with me, and keep me from harm so that I will be free from pain.' And God granted his request."* 1 Chronicles 4:9-10

For most people, the birth of a child is the most joyous of all occasions. After months of waiting, there is much celebration as you get to hold your baby for the very first time. Everything about that moment is special beyond words. In the Jewish culture, women longed to get married and give birth. We can see this longing through people like Sarah, Rachel and Elizabeth. Furthermore, many wished for a son to continue their family line.

In 1 Chronicles, in the middle of a list of names, we are introduced to Jabez. His birth should have been a moment of great rejoicing. His mother had given birth to a baby boy: the dream of every Jewish mother. Rather than celebrating, she calls her son Jabez meaning "sorrow" or "trouble." Instead of his birth becoming a source of joy to his mother, it was a source of pain, sorrow, disappointment, and trouble.

Sadly, there are still many children born today with the knowledge that they are unwanted by their parents. They are made to feel like an inconvenience and source of misfortune to their parent's lives. Some parents make their children feel that everything wrong in life is their child's fault. Maybe you have even experienced an element of this in your life.

Jabez lived with an embarrassing name that let the world know his birth caused pain and sorrow to his family. We only need to look around us to see how children who feel unwanted normally respond. Some turn to unhelpful peer groups, bad relationships, or drinking and drugs to try and find a sense of belonging to ease the pain of parental neglect.

Jabez was different. He turned to God for hope and prayed what has become one of the most famous short prayers in the whole Bible: *"Oh, that you would bless me and enlarge my territory! Let your hand be with me, and keep me from harm so that I will be free from pain."* Jabez asked God to bless him. The man who had always been neglected did not know what it was to be blessed or be a blessing. Even his own mother thought he was a curse, yet he turns to God from whom all blessings flow.

Jabez also asks God to enlarge his territories. He has been restricted his whole life, but he knows God has more for his life. Jabez' prayer is not born out of selfish desire, but because he wanted to honor God with his life. The words *"Let your hand be with me, and keep me from harm"* really means "keep me from evil." Jabez is asking God to protect him from moral depravity, corruption, and sinful desires that He may live a life of praise to God.

Jabez was born unloved. Everyone knew that he was unloved, but when he cried out to God, God granted his request. Do you feel forsaken by many, including those closest to you? Do you feel you are living a life less than what God wants for you? This short passage about Jabez remind us that God listens to the prayers of the abandoned and loves with unconditional love.

God took Jabez life from a place of pain and transformed it. There is only one other reference to Jabez. 1 Chronicles 2:55 says Jabez made so great an impact for God that the people around him decided his name must never be forgotten. Consequently, they built a city and populated it with families of scribes.

Today, be encouraged that your future is in God's hands. Even if you feel you have no hope and no future, you too can turn to God and, like Jabez, simply pray with confidence that God will hear you.

Related Passages:

1. 1 Chronicles 4:9

2. Jeremiah 29:11

Day 29
The Roman Centurion – God Softens the Hardened Murder

Key Passage: *"When the centurion and those with him who were guarding Jesus saw the earthquake and all that had happened, they were terrified, and exclaimed, 'Surely he was the Son of God!'"* Matthew 27:54

We do not know the name of the Roman Centurion who crucified Jesus, but we do know a lot about the man. In order to become a centurion, he must have been a tough, experienced warrior in the Roman Army. He would have been active in many of Rome's wars as they expanded their empire around the known world. He had likely seen and killed many, both on the battlefield and in his role of executioner in Israel under the rule of Pontius Pilate.

The Roman Centurion was a man used to death and killing. He probably did not even flinch as the nails were driven into hands which previously had blessed little children, healed the sick, multiplied bread, and raised the dead. As the nails were hammered into feet which had walked upon the water, the centurion was 'just doing his job.' As the cross was lifted up, and Jesus cried out in agony, the centurion was 'just following his orders.' He felt no shame in what he was doing.

We must recognize that while the centurion passively watched while nails were hammered into Jesus' hands, it was our sin and Jesus love for us that kept him on the cross. Each one of us is responsible for the crucifixion of Christ. I've read that in Mel Gibson's film *The Passion of Christ* he made a cameo appearance by using his hand to drive in the nails as a symbol of the fact that [Gibson] holds himself accountable first and foremost for Christ's death. The writer of the Hebrews also warns us that those *"who have tasted the goodness of the word of God and the powers of the coming age and who have fallen away... are crucifying the Son of God all over again and subjecting him to public disgrace."*[1] For the centurion, this was just another crucifixion until he recognized who Jesus was. He knew that Jesus claimed to be the son of God, yet he did not believe until he saw the darkness and earthquakes that accompanied Jesus' death. Have you recognized Jesus for who He is?

I imagine the centurion had never heard anyone pray before for them, let alone ask God to forgive them.[2] Most people probably only threw insults and hatred to the men who were torturing and executing them, but Jesus showed them love and compassion. Romans 5:10 teaches, *"For if, while we were God's enemies, we were reconciled to him through the death of his Son, how much more, having been reconciled, shall we be saved through his life!"* Each one of us had a time in our lives when we were God's enemies. When we think back on the things we have done and the decisions we have made, it is easy to conclude that God would never choose anyone like us. We may not have picked up the hammer to drive the nails into Jesus' hands, but Isaiah 53:5 reminds us, *"He was pierced for our transgressions, he was crushed for our iniquities; the punishment that brought us peace was on him, and by his wounds we are healed."*

The centurion's eyes were opened to his own failings. Moreover, by Jesus power and grace, he exclaimed, *"Surely he was the Son of God!"* Inspired by the Holy Spirit, the gospel writers took his words and embedded them into Scripture as a living testimony of who Jesus is. In a matter of hours, Jesus transformed the hardened executioner into a witness of his divinity for all of time. Regardless of what we have said or done to Jesus, his grace is powerful enough to transform our lives, so that we too may become a testimony of his love.

Related Passages:

1. Hebrews 6:5-6

2. Luke 23:34

Day 30
Lazarus – God Vanquishes Death

Key Passage: *"So then he told them plainly, 'Lazarus is dead, and for your sake I am glad I was not there, so that you may believe. But let us go to him.'"* John 11:14-15

Together over the past month, we have considered many people whom God used throughout the Bible. We have seen that many of them were unlikely choices from a human perspective. Hopefully, this has been of great encouragement to you, because God still uses the unlikely and He desires to use your life for his glory. Today we are going to finish this series by considering the most unlikely of all people for God to use. Whatever obstacles you think hinder you from being used by God, they pale compared to Lazarus. He was dead!

Jesus would often visit Mary, Martha, and Lazarus at their home on the Mount of Olives. In Luke 10, we have the scene where Martha was distracted by preparations for the visitors while Mary was spending time listening to Jesus. Clearly, Jesus had a close relationship with this family because when Lazarus got sick, the sisters send word to Jesus telling him that he one he loves is sick.[1] Jesus loved this family.

The family hoped that Jesus would rush back and heal Lazarus, but Jesus kept in tune with his Father's perfect timing. When he finally arrives at their house, Mary and Martha are in mourning and Lazarus is dead and has been buried for four days.[2] His body had already begun to decompose, and the odor soaked out from behind the stone.

Can you think of anyone less likely to be used by God? There are probably very few, if any, who read this who have experienced physical death. Yet, the Bible tells us in Ephesians 2:1 we were all *dead in our transgressions and sins.* We may not have experienced physical death, but spiritually each one of us was dead in our transgressions and sins. We were separate from God and as useful as a decomposing corpse.

As Lazarus' sisters mourned, Jesus spoke these beautiful words: *"I am the resurrection and the life. The one who believes in me will live, even though they die; and whoever lives by believing in me will never die. Do you believe this?"*[5] Jesus walks over to the grave, tells them to remove the stone, and calls for Lazarus to come out of his own grave. To the shock and joy of everyone, Lazarus walks out of the tomb.[6] The very next verse says, *"Therefore many of the Jews who had come to visit Mary, and had seen what Jesus did, believed in him."* In the following chapter we read *"the chief priests made plans to kill Lazarus, for on account of him many of the Jews were going over to Jesus and believing in him."*

Lazarus was dead in the grave, but three words from Jesus breathed life into him again while simultaneously bringing many souls into the Kingdom. The people of Israel wanted to see the man who God had moved from death into life. Today people are still desperate to see others living by God's resurrecting power. If you are a believer, this too is your testimony. God has taken you from death into life. We are alive by Christ' resurrection power, and our testimony should be evident for all to see.

Related Passages:

1. John 11:3

2. John 11:39

3. Ephesians 2:1

4. Romans 5:12

5. John 11:25-26

6. John 11:43-44

7. John 12:9-11

Thank you

Thank you for reading until the end of this book. I really hope that you've been encouraged that you are exactly the type of person that God wants to use.

If you enjoyed these devotions, you may also like to head over to my website at **www.jtdyer.com** and sign up to receive free my free daily devotional by email. Feel free to also reach out to me via the contact form. I'd love to hear from you.

If you found these devotionals helpful. It would really bless me if you could recommend them to others. One way to do that is to post a quick review on Amazon.

Thanks again, and may God bless you in all you do for His glory.

Blessings,
Jon

23905855R00065

Printed in Great Britain
by Amazon